ABUNDANT TRUTH INTERNATIONAL MINISTRIES

C.O.G.I.C. Protocols Series

THE MINISTRY OF THE ELDER

Practical Guidelines for Ordained C.O.G.I.C. Ministers

Roderick Levi Evans

The Ministry of the Elder
Practical Guidelines for Ordained C.O.G.I.C. Ministers

All Rights Reserved ©2022 Roderick L. Evans

No part of this book may be reproduced or transmitted in any form or by any means, graphic, electronic, or mechanical, including photocopying, recording, taping, or by any information storage or retrieval system, without the permission in writing from the publisher.

Abundant Truth Publishing
an imprint of Abundant Truth International Ministries
For information address:
Abundant Truth International
P.O. Box 126
Camden, NC 27921

Unless otherwise indicated, all of the scripture quotations are taken from the *Authorized King James Version* of the Bible. Scripture quotations marked with NIV are taken from the *New International Version* of the Bible. Scripture quotations marked with NASV are taken from the *New American Standard Version* of the Bible. Scripture quotations marked with Amplified are taken from the *Amplified Bible*.

ISBN 13: 9798293739844

Printed in the United States of America

Disclaimer: The information presented is not officially endoresed by the Church or any Jurisidiction, but provided as a supplement to the established order and protocols of C.O.G.I.C.

Contents

Introduction

Section 1 - Elders in the New Testament   1

The Classification of Elders   3
The Responsibility of Elder   11
The Lifestyle of Elders   15

Section 2 - Elders and the Church of God in Christ   27

The Ecclesiastical Structure   29
Specialized Ministries   34
Women & Eldership   35
Elders and the Denomination   38

Section 3 - Elders and the Jurisdictional Structure   43

The Role of the Bishop   46

Contents (cont.)

The Role of the Superintendent	47
The Role of the local Pastor	49
Jurisdictional Council of Pastors and Elders	50

Section 4 - Elders and the Local Pastor — 57

Aaron and the Priesthood	61
Moses and the Seventy	65
Korah's Rebellion	71
The Elder and Preaching Appointments	76

Section 5 — 85
Elders and the Local Church

The Example of David	88
The Ephesian Principle	93

Contents (cont.)

The Error of Joshua   99

Section 6 - Elders and the Pastorate   **109**
Recognizing the Call   112
Respect Leadership   117
Receiving the Appointment   121

Section 7 - Basic Protocols for the Ruling Elder   **129**
Seek Counsel   131
Have a Vision   133
Legal Accountability   138

Introduction

The Church of God in Christ is a church built on spiritual principles and practices. The church is known for its order and respect of its leaders.

The C.O.G.I.C. Protocols Series is developed to help those within the church execute their duties and ministries within the standards set by the church.

In this publication

In this publication, we will discuss the ministry of the C.O.G.I.C. Elder. It is our endeavor to help those entering the ministry by having supplemental support as they navigate the execution of their ministries. In addition, we will provide basic protocols for the Elder's purpose and function.

THE MINISTRY OF THE ELDER

-Section 1-

Elders in the New Testament

THE MINISTRY OF THE ELDER

THE MINISTRY OF THE ELDER

The ministry and role of the Elder is clearly established throughout the New Testament writings. To effectively discharge his duty, the Elder must have a firm grasp on his spiritual heritage and significance.

In this opening section, we will look at the ministry and function of Elders in the early Church, which form the foundation for his ministry today and within C.O.G.I.C.

The Classification of Elders

The New Testament reveals that God set ministries in the Church at its inception to ensure its spiritual success and growth. As Paul called for peace and unity in the Corinthian church, he established this truth.

Now ye are the body of Christ, and members in particular. And God hath set some in the church, first apostles, secondarily prophets, thirdly teachers, after that miracles, then gifts of healings, helps, governments, diversities of tongues. (I Cor. 12:27-28)

However, we discover that as the

THE MINISTRY OF THE ELDER

Church grew, there was an ever-increasing need for localized leadership. Paul, therefore, gave instructions on how this was to be done.

In his writings to Timothy and Titus, we discover that bishops and pastors were appointed to exercise spiritual and ecclesiastical authority over the flock of God.

> *For this cause left I thee in Crete, that thou shouldest set in order the things that are wanting, and ordain elders in every city, as I had appointed thee. (Titus 1:5)*

THE MINISTRY OF THE ELDER

In the New Testament model, any man called to the ministry of preaching was appointed and recognized as an Elder.

Even those who were called specifically as apostles, prophets, evangelists, pastors, and teachers were recognized as Elders in apostolic times. Peter, though he was an apostle, called himself an Elder as well.

The elders which are among you I exhort, who am also an elder, and a witness of the sufferings of Christ, and also a partaker of the glory that shall be revealed. (I Peter 5:1)

THE MINISTRY OF THE ELDER

Within the local assemblies, Elders could then be appointed as bishops. All Elders were not pastors, neither were all pastors appointed as bishops. In the Antioch church, they had numerous Elders, who were there, but only Paul and Barnabas were set aside for a greater work.

Now there were in the church that was at Antioch certain prophets and teachers; as Barnabas, and Simeon that was called Niger, and Lucius of Cyrene, and Manaen, which had been brought up with Herod the tetrarch, and Saul. As they ministered to the Lord, and fasted, the Holy Ghost said, Separate me Barnabas and Saul for the work whereunto I have called them. 3And when they had fasted and prayed, and laid their hands on them, they sent them away. (Acts 13:1-3)

We want to pause here to make an important statement. **Every Elder may not be called to become a pastor. Every pastor may not be appointed as a superintendent and/or bishop.** When the Elder understands his scope and measure

THE MINISTRY OF THE ELDER

of ministry, he will be able to operate at his fullest potential without hindrance, contention, or controversy. To clarify our position, we have developed three classifications for the ministry of the Elder within C.O.G.I.C.

1) **Servant Elder** – The Elder who serves a local pastor and church. The local church becomes the main area of the execution of his ministry.*

2) **Evangelist Elder** – The Elder who has a duality in ministry. He serves a local pastor and church as well as has an established itinerate ministry

THE MINISTRY OF THE ELDER

whether its emphasis is evangelism, prophetic, or teaching.*

3) **Ruling Elder** – The Elder who is a pastor, having the oversight of an organized Body of believers. Pastors, superintendents, and bishops can all be classified as Ruling Elders.

*Elders in this classification may become pastors one day. However, until that time, the Elder's ministry will fall into one of these designations.

The ministers in the New Testament endeavored for the peace, unity, and spiritual growth of the Church regardless

THE MINISTRY OF THE ELDER

of his ministerial classification (whether elder, pastor, or bishop).

There was a classification of Elders in the New Testament, which forms the foundation for the classification of Elders in C.O.G.I.C.

The Responsibility of Elders

We have already established that Elders in the New Testament were appointed for the spiritual well-being and growth of the Church. The same is true for the Elder today.

As we proceed further in this book, we will discuss the relationship between

THE MINISTRY OF THE ELDER

the pastor (Elder with charge) and Ordained Ministers (Elder without charge) as they serve in the local church.

However, in this section, we want to address the general responsibilities of Elders (regardless of classification).

Elders must be carriers of the gospel of Jesus Christ. He must have the ability to defend the faith, not just present an exciting "sermon."

The Elder must be doctrinally sound in New Testament theology as well as understand the articles of faith of the C.O.G.I.C. faith.

THE MINISTRY OF THE ELDER

Elders must be chief servants. Jesus challenged his disciples by reminding them that an anointing to lead comes with a mandate to serve.

But ye shall not be so: but he that is greatest among you, let him be as the younger; and he that is chief, as he that doth serve. For whether is greater, he that sitteth at meat, or he that serveth? is not he that sitteth at meat? but I am among you as he that serveth. (Luke 22:26-27)

Elders should be supporters (spiritually and financially) of the

national and local church. They should also be chief supporters of established leadership. Local Elders should be servants and supporters of the local pastor. Pastors should be supporters of the superintendent.

Superintendents should be supporters and garners of support of the Jurisdictional Bishop, and so on. This reveals that Elders must lead by example, demonstrating how to exercise authority and be under authority.

Elders must act as spiritual protectors of the churches. Their ministries should preserve doctrinal purity and guard against spiritual deception from entering the Church. They must be men of prayer, exercising spiritual discernment and authority.

The Lifestyle of Elders

Elders must live according to godly principles and be holy men of God. The Official Manual deems that those ordained as Elders must have lifestyles befitting ministers of the gospel.

Though these things are outlined in the scriptures, we found it necessary to address the lifestyle qualities of the Elder.

THE MINISTRY OF THE ELDER

Holiness should be the foundation for the Elder's ministry. The lifestyle requirements of the Elder (regardless of classification) is outlined in I Timothy 3:2-7.

A. Blameless - The Elder has to be blameless. This does not mean that he is without fault and cannot make mistakes. It does mean that an elder cannot be known or identified with a particular sin.

B. Husband of One Wife – Elders have to be examples in their personal lives. This exhortation is a direct prohibition against polygamy. Yet, it has a greater implication. A pastor's personal life has to reflect proper moral conduct that compliments the gospel. Thus, this exhortation speaks to faithfulness in marriage and against any sexual misconduct.

C. Vigilant - Elders have to possess vigilance. Vigilance speaks to the Elder's faithfulness in the execution of the ministry. Every Elder must be faithful to the call of God. He must demonstrate loyalty to Christ and the Church.

D. Sober – An Elder has to be sober in judgment and character. Paul is not referring to sobriety in terms of alcohol, but in demonstration and execution of the ministry. Pastors cannot be foolish and immature. They must demonstrate godly and sound wisdom in their lives.

E. Good Behavior - Elders are to exhibit good behavior. Elders have to exercise patience and kindness as they minister to the Church. Elders are not to be "task masters" over the people of God. They must exercise longsuffering as they execute their ministries. They have to demonstrate compassion and faithfulness as they interact with the

THE MINISTRY OF THE ELDER

Body of Christ.

F. Given to Hospitality - Every Elder has to be approachable. Paul exhorted Timothy to look for those who know how to entreat others. Some Elders only interact with believers from the pulpit. However, hospitality is to be demonstrated outside of the location of the Church.

G. Apt to Teach - Elders have to be willing to instruct others as the need arises. They ought to understand the foundational truths of the faith and be willing to share with others at all times.

THE MINISTRY OF THE ELDER

They have to be willing to teach with the right attitude also. They must have the right words with the proper delivery. It is a required trait of the servant of the Lord.

H. Not given to wine - Elders should not be under the influence of alcoholic substances. They should not be drunkards. In addition, Elders should not be under the influence of any intoxicating substance, which includes drugs (illegal or prescription).

I. Not a striker, Not a brawler – Elders are not to engage in verbal and physical conflicts. They are not to be argumentative. They are to hold the truth in love. They are not to have bad attitudes and harsh demeanors. Again, they are not to resolve any disputes (professional, personal, and ministerial) with the use of physical violence. Self-control is needed in the pulpit, on the mission field, or in their homes.

J. Not Greedy for Money or Covetous – Elders should not preach and teach for money. They will be motivated by a love for the Church and obedience to Christ. In addition, they will not be covetous for material gain and vain recognition. Elders should never use their office to become rich.

K. Patient - Patience is one of the identifiable marks of a good Elder. Elders have to be men of patience as they minister to the Church. Patience is vital for this ministry. Elders must have patience as they wait to see the fruits of their labors develop in the lives of believers. They must exercise patience as they execute their ministries.

L. Rules own house well – An Elder should know how to lead his family. He should

THE MINISTRY OF THE ELDER

have the respect and support of his wife and children. The exhortation is simple, if he does not know how to govern his own house; he will be ineffective in the pastoral office.

Now that we have established the role of Elders in the New Testament and addressed general duties of the Elder, and reviewed the lifestyle requirements, we want to turn our attention more specifically to the Elder, understanding his place, role, and function within C.O.G.I.C.

THE MINISTRY OF THE ELDER

Ministerial Notes:

_____

_____

_____

_____

_____

_____

_____

_____

THE MINISTRY OF THE ELDER

-Section 2-

Elders and the Church of God in Christ, Inc.

THE MINISTRY OF THE ELDER

The C.O.G.I.C. faith endeavors to be biblically based and culturally relevant. Both of these considerations were in view as the structure for the Church and its organizational structure and protocols were instituted.

In this section, we want to give a brief examination of the role of the Elder within C.O.G.I.C. and understand its basis. For a full examination of these things, please refer to the Official Manual.

The Ecclesiastical Structure

The C.O.G.I.C. faith utilizes a biblical model for its ecclesiastical structure. In the

THE MINISTRY OF THE ELDER

New Testament, there is a distinction made between ecclesiastical structure and spiritual functions and offices. Oftentimes these are confused and some feel that the C.O.G.I.C. structure is not scripturally valid, but this is not true.

The ministry offices listed in Ephesians 4 are not given as an ecclesiastical structure, but to demonstrate that within that structure, these offices will be in operation. Remember, Peter referred to himself as an Elder. Apostles, prophets, pastors, evangelists, and teachers are Elders.

Therefore, when Paul lists these gifts, he had in mind that the Elders that were appointed in the Churches would possess these endowments given by Christ, since they are necessary for the spiritual growth, maturity, and protection of the Church.

And he gave some, apostles; and some, prophets; and some, evangelists; and some, pastors and teachers; For the perfecting of the saints, for the work of the ministry, for the edifying of the body of Christ: Till we all come in the unity of the faith, and of the knowledge of

THE MINISTRY OF THE ELDER

the Son of God, unto a perfect man, unto the measure of the stature of the fullness of Christ: hat we henceforth be no more children, tossed to and fro, and carried about with every wind of doctrine, by the sleight of men, and cunning craftiness, whereby they lie in wait to deceive (Ephesians 4:11-14)

So, within the C.O.G.I.C. faith, we follow the example of the apostles who appointed bishops, pastors, and leaders as the model for ecclesiastical structure. In

THE MINISTRY OF THE ELDER

the Official Manual, there is a clear explanation of the relationship between the spiritual offices in relation to the ecclesiastical offices. Ecclesiastical appointments are in and approved endorsement of all ministry leaders.

In brief, C.O.G.I.C. follows the ecclesiastical heritage of appointing bishops, pastors, and ordained ministers – all of which are referred to as Elders, regardless of which spiritual endowments may be upon them.

These are given for oversight, protection, and to bring spiritual order to

THE MINISTRY OF THE ELDER

the operation of Church on the local, district, jurisdictional, and national levels.

Specialized Ministries

We have previously stated that regardless of one's ministry function as apostle, prophet, evangelist, pastor, or teacher, he is considered an Elder based upon New Testament examples.

Within C.O.G.I.C., though we recognize the operation of these ministries and offices, ordination to all of these specific offices is not a standard practice of C.O.G.I.C.

Those who operate in a specialized

THE MINISTRY OF THE ELDER

ministry such as evangelist or teacher should not feel that the ordination as Elder is in anyway a devaluation of that particular ministry. Rather, the ordination as Elder is a direct acknowledgment of God's anointing upon you.

The Elder must endeavor to fulfill the function of that specialized ministry, if by chance, a certain title is not afforded him.

Women & Eldership

Since C.O.G.I.C. endeavors to maintain biblical congruity in establishing its ministerial structure, we hold certain protocols for women in ministry. C.O.G.I.C.

THE MINISTRY OF THE ELDER

recognizes the spiritual gifts and ministries of women, however, no clear biblical examples of the apostles appointing women as bishops, elders, and pastors are given.

Hence, C.O.G.I.C. does not ordain women as Elders. It is not a gender-biased and/or male chauvinist decision, but one founded solely upon biblical precedence.

Although C.O.G.I.C. does not ordain women into Ecclesiastical ministry, women are allowed to minister in other areas without prohibition. Women are licensed as Missionaries in C.O.G.I.C. to facilitate

THE MINISTRY OF THE ELDER

their God-given ministries, locally and abroad.

We know from biblical examples vthat women could preach, prophesy, and serve in leadership positions, being appointed by ecclesiastical leadership. This is the model that C.O.G.I.C. endeavors to preserve and adhere to.

Although other reformations appoint women to ecclesiastical offices such as bishop, elder, and pastor, the Elder in C.O.G.I.C. must understand that we do not promote such practices within the Church. Please refer to the Official Manual, for a

THE MINISTRY OF THE ELDER

full explanation of the role of women in ministry within C.O.G.I.C.

Elders and the Denomination

Becoming an Elder in C.O.G.I.C. comes with certain rules, regulations, and prohibitions. These are not designed to control, but to bring order and preserve the Elder and the Church.

Ordination within C.O.G.I.C. is an agreement between the Elder and the denomination that the Elder will adhere and promote the principles of the Church. Though this should be understood, but history has shown that some do not

THE MINISTRY OF THE ELDER

understand that this is a requirement and not a suggestion.

An ordained minister (Elder) upon his reception of the appointment becomes, in effect, the property of the denomination.

This means that his ministry and manner of living becomes subject to the established leadership as long as he holds credentials within the denomination. Hence, his lifestyle is subject to review, correction, and discipline, as outlined in the Official Manual.

THE MINISTRY OF THE ELDER

This concept of his being the property of the denomination extends until the day of his transition to the heavenly hope.

The Elder without charge serves the local church at the discretion of the local pastor. He must be ready to serve his district. In addition, he also must be ready to serve in any capacity as deemed necessary by the Jurisdictional Bishop.

THE MINISTRY OF THE ELDER

Ministerial Notes:

THE MINISTRY OF THE ELDER

-Section 3-

Elders and the Jurisdictional Structure

THE MINISTRY OF THE ELDER

THE MINISTRY OF THE ELDER

Elders need to be acquainted with the basic organizational structure of the church. Though one who is ordained should have a working knowledge of these things, we thought it necessary to review, briefly, organizational structure and authority.

The national church is led by the presiding Chief Apostle along with the twelve bishops for the overall governance of C.O.G.I.C.

After this, the churches are organized into jurisdictions (led by bishops) and more acutely into districts (led by

THE MINISTRY OF THE ELDER

superintendents), and then local churches (governed by local pastors).

All of this information is included in the Official Manual. With this is mind, we will look briefly at the roles of authority in this structure, and how it affects the Elder.

The Role of the Bishop

Bishops are appointed by the presiding prelate of C.O.G.I.C. to govern jurisdictions. The bishop oversees all of the pastors and churches within the jurisdictional boundaries. He alone ordains ministers as Elders.

THE MINISTRY OF THE ELDER

He also sets Elders into the pastoral office. He also appoints superintendents over the districts within the jurisdiction.

He also oversees the placement of all jurisdictional officers as well as appoint jurisdictional officials. Moreover, he conducts the funerals of all pastors, elders, and jurisdictional officials. The bishop is the jurisdictional leader who represents the voice of the C.O.G.I.C., both inside and outside of the church.

The Role of the Superintendent

Superintendents are appointed over districts by the jurisdictional bishop. The

THE MINISTRY OF THE ELDER

superintendent oversees the pastors and churches in his district. He oversees the placements and appointment of district officials.

He presides over the annual district conference and all meetings of pastors and elders in his district.

He keeps the local pastors informed concerning any directives from the jurisdictional bishop and keeps support for the jurisdiction vibrant and active. He mediates any issues that may arise concerning the pastors in his district.

THE MINISTRY OF THE ELDER

The Role of the local Pastor

The jurisdictional bishop installs pastors. They are the authority for the governance and spiritual oversight of the local church. He provides spiritual direction and support for the members of his church.

He is the chair of all business meetings conducted by the local church (except he appoints a substitute when needed). Any conflicts with members should be brought to his care and oversight.

The local pastor also keeps the local

THE MINISTRY OF THE ELDER

congregants informed of any directives given by the district superintendent. The pastor appoints and oversees the placement of ALL ministries and auxiliaries in his church. He has the sole authority to remove any officers and leaders of his local church as deemed necessary.

All local Elders are subject to the leadership of the local pastor where they have membership.

Jurisdictional Council of Pastors and Elders

(Brief overview taken directly from the "General Council of Pastors and Elders

THE MINISTRY OF THE ELDER

"Official Handbook" – Governing Rules, Regulations, and Procedures")

Every ordained Elder in good standing with his local church and ecclesiastical jurisdiction makes up this group. It is led by an elected chairman.

The purpose of the Jurisdictional Council of Pastors and Elders is to ensure and protect the rights and privileges of the pastors and elders in the Jurisdiction.

In addition, it ensures that they understand the relationship between their role as pastors and elders

THE MINISTRY OF THE ELDER

with that of the jurisdictional bishop's authority under whom they serve, including their duties, responsibilities, obligations, liability, and accountability.

The function of the jurisdictional council is two-fold. First, it serves as the trial court for the jurisdiction. It also serves as a training institute. This council shall also carry out other duties delegated to it by **Article V, Section B** of the Constitution of the Church of God in Christ. This council meets twice annually at the Jurisdictional Holy Convocation and the Jurisdictional Worker's Meeting.

THE MINISTRY OF THE ELDER

It may also hold other conferences and meetings as needed. Every Elder should plan to attend all scheduled and called meetings of this council.

For more information, please consult the official handbook of this council, available from the General Council of Pastors and Elders of the national church.

The Elder has to have a working knowledge of order and protocol. If an issue arises in a local church, the pastor is to be consulted first. From there, the pastor contacts his superintendent.

THE MINISTRY OF THE ELDER

The superintendent makes contact with the bishop and jurisdictional officials if a matter necessitates their personal involvement. The Elder who has the protocols of authority in place will do well.

THE MINISTRY OF THE ELDER

Ministerial Notes:

_____

_____

_____

_____

_____

_____

_____

_____

THE MINISTRY OF THE ELDER

-Section 4-
Elders and the Local Pastor

THE MINISTRY OF THE ELDER

Having established the basis for the ministry of the Elder and establishing the jurisdictional structure, the minister must know how to function within his local church. Though much available information for the pastor is available, the Elder who is not the shepherd lacks some instruction among C.O.G.I.C. clergy.

In this section and those to follow, we will now turn our attention to the ministries of the Servant Elder and/or Evangelist Elder (see page 9); that is, the ordained minister who currently do not

THE MINISTRY OF THE ELDER

occupy the office of pastor. Tension, confusion, and division are potential threats to the harmony between the Elder and the local pastor.

If the Elder understands his role and function within the local church and his position in respect to the local pastor, it will result in a fruitful, flourishing ministry of the Elder himself, the pastor, and the local Church.

Before examining the particular functions of the Elder, we will address the Elder's relationship with the local pastor. Through biblical examples, we will

THE MINISTRY OF THE ELDER

establish the proper attitude and approach to the interaction with the local pastor.

Though the ordained minister is an Elder as is the local pastor, he must understand that there are fundamental and intrinsic differences between them with respect to the operation, leadership, and governance of the local church.

Aaron and the Priesthood

Under the Old Covenant, the Lord instituted the Aaronic (Levitical) Priesthood (Leviticus 8). Within this group, there was the high priest, the priesthood, the singers, the porters, and all who had

THE MINISTRY OF THE ELDER

service in the house of the Lord. However, it is discovered that though many priests served, there was only **one** High Priest who had the authority from God to perform certain duties and rituals.

Likewise, within the New Testament church, all believers are part of Christ's royal priesthood. However, not all believers are called to a preaching or teaching ministry. In addition, all those called to a preaching and teaching ministry, will not pastor a church.

Though they will have to carry out many of the responsibilities and actions of

THE MINISTRY OF THE ELDER

those in the pastorate, the difference is the authority given to the pastor by the Church and from Christ.

Remember in the book of Revelation, Christ told John to direct his prophecies to the "angel" of each church; that is, the pastor.

Unto the angel of the church... write... (Revelation 2:1)

We know these churches had other leaders within the Church, but because the ultimate responsibility is given to the pastor, Christ directed His words to them in particular.

THE MINISTRY OF THE ELDER

The Elder must understand that though he is ecclesiastically licensed as an Elder, within that local assembly, he is subject to the pastor, giving proper respect to him as deemed fit by Christ and established church leadership. Israel had many priests, but only one high priest. The local church may have numerous Elders, but there is only one pastor.

The Elder must understand that it is an issue of ecclesiastical and spiritual authority. The Elder, then, must discharge his duties with respect to the vision established by that leadership and operate

THE MINISTRY OF THE ELDER

within the liberty that the local pastor grants him.

Again, the Elder must respect and submit to the authority of the pastor to ensure peace and harmony in the leadership of the local Church.

Moses and the Seventy

We have heard this expression, "Have the spirit of your leader." However, do we understand the basis for it? It is something that every Elder should have in mind with regard to the local pastor.

Whether a church has two members or two thousand members; there will be

THE MINISTRY OF THE ELDER

many needs, and the leadership of the Church should have one sound, one voice, and one manner to effectively meet the needs of the people. Moses encountered this same problem. The congregation of Israel was many, hence, the Lord told him to choose seventy men.

> *And the LORD said unto Moses, Gather unto me seventy men of the elders of Israel, whom thou knowest to be the elders of the people, and officers over them; and bring them unto the tabernacle of the congregation, that they may*

stand there with thee. And I will come down and talk with thee there: and I will take of the spirit which is upon thee, and will put it upon them; and they shall bear the burden of the people with thee, that thou bear it not thyself alone. (Numbers 11:16-17)

Moses' choice was not to be made lightly. Men, recognized as leaders were to be chosen. However, they were not going to take on Moses' personal character traits but partake of his anointing to help govern the people.

THE MINISTRY OF THE ELDER

Every Elder should pray and ask for a portion of their pastor's spirit to effectively help the progress of the local Church, even if that Elder will never pastor or has a focused ministry in another area such as evangelism.

If one is to serve effectively as an Elder, he must understand, he will need a portion of the pastor's spirit so that the congregation can receive proper pastoral care when the pastor is physically absent.

Doing so, will not rob the Elder of his personal ministry, but enhance it. Remember, Elisha was already going to be

THE MINISTRY OF THE ELDER

prophet in Elijah's stead, but he asked for a double portion of Elijah's spirit, which was manifested in the many miracles he performed.

The Elder who thinks he is complete within himself concerning his service in the local church is deceived. Since he is not the pastor, he will need spiritual insight to ensure that his preaching, counsel, and service is on one accord with the pastor. When Paul could not reach the Corinthian church, he sent Titus, look at his words,

> *I desired Titus, and with him I sent a brother. Did Titus make a gain of*

you? walked we not in the same spirit? walked we not in the same steps? (2 Corinthians 12:18)

Titus was a man of God with his own ministry in particular. However, Paul sent Titus to the church and could boast that Titus did not do anything aside from what he would do if he were there personally. The ministry of the Elder in the local church should resemble this in relation to the pastor.

The Elder's ministry to the local Church should be an extension of the established pastoral ministry.

THE MINISTRY OF THE ELDER

Korah's Rebellion

We began this section explaining the difference between the Elder and the local pastor by establishing it as an issue of authority. Since ego and pride are enemies of any person in ministry, we want to solidify biblically, the Lord's perspective to differences of authority among ministers though all stand before Him equally.

God chose Moses and Aaron to lead Israel. They were from the tribe of Levi, but God had made choice of Moses as His prophet and Aaron as the High Priest for that time. However, other Levites (who

THE MINISTRY OF THE ELDER

were also separated unto the service of the Lord) had gotten upset and accused Moses and Aaron of usurping all of the authority over the people.

Now Korah, the son of Izhar, the son of Kohath, the son of Levi, and Dathan and Abiram, the sons of Eliab, and On, the son of Peleth, sons of Reuben, took men: And they rose up before Moses, with certain of the children of Israel, two hundred and fifty princes of the assembly, famous in the congregation, men of renown: And they gathered themselves together against Moses and against Aaron, and said unto them, Ye take too much upon you, seeing all the congregation are holy, every one of them, and the LORD is among them: wherefore then lift ye up yourselves above the congregation of the LORD? (Numbers 16:1-3)

We know how this story ended; God judged Korah and destroyed the Levites who challenged Aaron. In addition, God caused Aaron's rod to bud. This story introduces us to some important points.

First, the Elder has to respect,

THE MINISTRY OF THE ELDER

sincerely, the leadership of the local church. He cannot be like Korah in thinking that the pastor is doing too much.

Some Elders think (like Korah) that the pastor is taking too much to himself if he chooses to preach every Sunday, do all the counseling, and teach all the bible studies. Each pastor has a different mandate of God and the local assembly may need more personal, pastoral input from the local pastor than others.

Elders must respect the liberty or lack of liberty a pastor gives to other ministers

THE MINISTRY OF THE ELDER

in the local Church. He must be mindful that the pastor may be under a divine mandate to be strict or lenient in terms of allowing others to speak and minister in the congregation.

An Elder must respect the ministerial guidelines for other ministers in the local church, established by the Pastor.

An Elder who is not sensitive to this can think that the pastor is selfish, not realizing that the pastor has been directed by the Spirit of God. Alternatively, some can think the Pastor should not allow others to minister, when he has been

THE MINISTRY OF THE ELDER

instructed to give liberty to others in the congregation to minister.

Consequently, the Elder can inadvertently oppose God and set himself up for unnecessary divine discipline, as did Korah.

The Elder and Preaching Appointments

The Elder has to possess the proper attitude if his ministry extends beyond the local assembly, whether he is a full-time itinerate (travelling) minister or he receives outside invitations to minister occasionally. The Elder must use wisdom, discretion, and be accountable to his local

THE MINISTRY OF THE ELDER

pastor. This demonstrates respect for the one who has the authority over you in ministry and humility.

An Elder has to subject the execution of his ministry to his pastor. Each pastor may be different as to how they facilitate the ministry of others.

Hence, some pastors are very liberal and have no restrictions to an Elder receiving outside appointments to minister. Conversely, some pastors may be more rigid in their protocols for Elders and ministers as they receive outside appointments.

THE MINISTRY OF THE ELDER

More plainly, some pastors require only to be notified of the engagements only. Others, however, may have the rule of asking permission from them before an appointment is accepted.

No one way is better than the other, but whatever that local pastor's stance is on the matter should be followed with humility and submission. Here are a few points the Elder must keep in mind.

1. If a pastor is liberal in his approach to Elders taking/receiving appointments, it is not to be taken advantage of. An Elder should never

THE MINISTRY OF THE ELDER

be away preaching or teaching without his pastor's knowledge and/or blessing. An Elder is always under authority even in the execution of his personal ministry.

2. If a pastor is more restrictive in his approach, Elders should not regard this as a hindrance, but rather as a protection and covering for their ministries and souls. The pastor's restrictions should never be disregarded, resulting in an Elder being rebellious taking / receiving appointments outside of the pastor's

THE MINISTRY OF THE ELDER

requirements or guidelines. In addition, the pastor's restrictions should never be complained about before others. Submission and humility should be the Elder's response.

The Elder that has the proper attitude toward his position in respect to the local pastor will make full proof of his ministry. In conclusion, the elder must:

1. *Realize the authority of the local pastor.*
2. *Receive a portion of the local pastor's spirit.*

THE MINISTRY OF THE ELDER

3. Respect the ministerial guidelines of the local pastor.

It contributes to the success of the pastor and local church and sets himself up for personal fruitful ministry whether as a future pastor, itinerate minister, or serving minister in the Church.

THE MINISTRY OF THE ELDER

THE MINISTRY OF THE ELDER

Ministerial Notes:

_____

_____

_____

_____

_____

_____

_____

_____

THE MINISTRY OF THE ELDER

-Section 5-
Elders and the Local Church

THE MINISTRY OF THE ELDER

When the Elder understands his relationship with the local pastor, his ministry to the local church will be blessed and beneficial. Having established the relationship between the Elder and the local pastor, we can focus on the parameters of the Elder's ministry to the local congregation.

We want to look at three biblical examples to bring definition to the Elder's service on the local level. The Servant Elder and/or Evangelist Elder (see page 9); must not only know his place with respect to the pastor, but also in relation to the

THE MINISTRY OF THE ELDER

congregation of which he is a member.

The Example of David

David's relationship with Saul is set forth as the standard for leaders in relation to other leaders. However, for our argument, we want to look at David's relationship with his father to establish truths concerning the Elder and the local assembly. When Goliath challenged the armies of Israel, David made an appeal to Saul to allow him to face Goliath in battle. Let us look closely at David's words.

And David said unto Saul, Thy servant kept his father's sheep, and

THE MINISTRY OF THE ELDER

there came a lion, and a bear, and took a lamb out of the flock: And I went out after him, and smote him, and delivered it out of his mouth: and when he arose against me, I caught him by his beard, and smote him, and slew him. (I Samuel 17:34-35)

David recalls how he kept his **father's sheep**, yet he risked his life to save them. David risked his life to save a lamb out of the flock, which did not personally belong to him. The Elder has to have the same love and approach to the

THE MINISTRY OF THE ELDER

local assembly. *The Elder must be a protector and defender of the local congregants.*

Though he does not exercise pastoral authority, he must love the flock of God; that is, the local parishioners as if they were his own and lay down his life as the pastor would. David protected his father's sheep and the Elder should protect his Pastor's flock seeing that all belong to the Lord.

*The Elder has to exercise the same concern and burden for the congregation as the pastor without

THE MINISTRY OF THE ELDER

having to receive the same recognition and authority as the pastor.

David saved the lamb and thought of it as his responsibility. The Elder's approach to the local assembly must be the same.

The Elder should have the spiritual health and care of the local congregants in mind. As he exercises his assigned duties and responsibilities, he should never cause others to hear him or respond to him above the local pastor.

He has to know how to minister effectively without developing a following.

THE MINISTRY OF THE ELDER

The Elder should not "preserve sheep" to himself.

As an Elder, you must not allow others to exalt you with flattery and tell you that they can talk to you and not the pastor. They may not mean any harm, but you will have to minister to them so that they can receive ministry from and have a relationship with the local pastor.

Never have your own congregation within a congregation. The Holy Spirit comes to unify and **NOT** to divide; and one of the central points of unity in a church is the local leadership.

THE MINISTRY OF THE ELDER

David did not save the lamb and then keep it for himself. He restored the lamb to his **father's** flock. The Elder must minister to the congregants that they remain vibrant members of the local flock under the leadership of the appointed spiritual father, which is the local pastor.

The Ephesian Principle

Elders consistently perform numerous functions as they serve the local pastor and minister in the local Church. Some serve as armor-bearers, counselors, teachers, youth ministers, prayer team members, administrators, assistants, and

THE MINISTRY OF THE ELDER

other areas of service. Regardless of the Elder's area of service, there must be a driving principle to his service. The exhortations of scripture should temper his ministry endeavors.

Paul's letter to the Ephesian church contained many foundational truths concerning the eternal purpose of God, the superior ministry of Christ, and the mystery of the Church, which is the body of Christ.

As he established these truths, Paul challenged the Ephesian church to remain unified.

THE MINISTRY OF THE ELDER

His appeal for unity, (we have designated) ***The Ephesian Principle***, should govern the activities of the Elder. The fourth chapter of this epistle details this principle.

I therefore, the prisoner of the Lord, beseech you that ye walk worthy of the vocation wherewith ye are called, With all lowliness and meekness, with longsuffering, forbearing one another in love; Endeavoring to keep the unity of the Spirit in the bond of peace. (Ephesians 4:1-3)

THE MINISTRY OF THE ELDER

These verses present the principle for ministry of the Elder in the local church.

1. **The Elder must walk worthy.** His lifestyle even among the congregants should be one that is commendable in terms of holiness and godly living. His godly lifestyle makes it easier for others to receive ministry that will come from him.

2. **The Elder must demonstrate meekness and lowliness.** He should not be arrogant because of his position, or prideful because of appointments

given by the local pastor.

His authority has to be tempered by true humility and meekness. In doing so, his ministry will be readily received and effective.

3. **The Elder must be patient and know how to put up with others by demonstrating the love of Christ.** Elders must have a pastoral spirit to navigate the differing personalities in the congregation without becoming angry, bitter, and judgmental of the congregants to which he has to execute ministry.

THE MINISTRY OF THE ELDER

4. **The Elder must always endeavor for the unity of the congregation.** The Elder should execute ministry with unity in mind. With many issues challenging the unity of an assembly, the Elder must know, through the wisdom of the Spirit, how to preserve unity when controversy and disagreements arise. His actions should never cause a split in the church, no matter how trivial a matter it is.

The Elder who will hold to the principles given to the Ephesian church will protect himself, the pastor, and the church against spiritual deception and division. These admonitions must govern his ministry to the local church.

The Error of Joshua

The Elder, we have discussed, must respect the local pastor and submit to his leadership. However, not every Elder has a problem with doing this.

Yet, even in respect, obedience, and submission to the local pastor there is a balance. To clarify our sentiments, we will look at our third biblical example.

Joshua is one of the greatest examples of leadership in training and also submission and loyalty to established

THE MINISTRY OF THE ELDER

leadership. He stood at the foot of the mount for forty days while Moses received the tablets with God's writing.

He was always loyal and faithful to Moses. He was even one of the twelve sent to spy out the Promised Land; being one of two who came back with a righteous and good report. However, his submission to Moses blinded him against the move of God.

In section 4, we discussed the Lord's instruction to Moses to choose seventy men that He could put Moses' spirit upon. In these events, we see Joshua's loyalty to

THE MINISTRY OF THE ELDER

Moses put him at odds with God.

After God placed Moses' spirit upon the seventy, two men were prophesying in the camp because of this endowment. Faithful, loyal Joshua did not appreciate this.

> *But there remained two of the men in the camp, the name of the one was Eldad, and the name of the other Medad: and the spirit rested upon them; and they were of them that were written, but went not out unto the tabernacle: and they prophesied in the camp. And there*

ran a young man, and told Moses, and said, Eldad and Medad do prophesy in the camp. And Joshua the son of Nun, the servant of Moses, one of his young men, answered and said, My lord Moses, forbid them. And Moses said unto him, Enviest thou for my sake? would God that all the LORD'S people were prophets, and that the LORD would put his spirit upon them! (Numbers 11:26-29)

Joshua felt that these men were out of order. However, they were only responding to what God was doing; for, they were chosen by Moses to receive this anointing. Moses' response to Joshua shows that Joshua felt that they were intruding into an area that they were not allowed; but he was wrong. Moses had to rebuke him.

As the Elder attempts to follow and submit to leadership and encourage others to do so, he cannot restrict what God will do through others under the leadership of the local pastor. Elders should not act as henchmen and enforcers of the local pastor, but rather as

endorsers of the pastor's authority, work, vision, and ministry.

What is the difference? One approach uses brutality, bullying, control, and scare tactics. The other approach keeps people mindful of the will of God and demonstrates how people should respond to the pastor through the Elder's example of submission and service.

When the pastor allows others in the congregation to minister, the Elders cannot speak against what the pastor endorses - in the name of allegiance to the pastor. They just verified that they are

THE MINISTRY OF THE ELDER

not in submission to him, if they speak against others whom he sets in place in ministries and auxiliaries.

This was Joshua's error. He was envious for Moses' sake; however, it put him at odds with Moses and the will of God. As the Elder protects the leadership, he must remember that it cannot be on personal terms, but according to the will of God.

The ministry of the Elder in the local church is important. If the Elder approaches it with godly motives and proper attitudes, his service to the local

THE MINISTRY OF THE ELDER

church will be indispensable, appreciated and valued by all, especially the local pastor.

THE MINISTRY OF THE ELDER

Ministerial Notes:

_____

_____

_____

_____

_____

_____

_____

_____

THE MINISTRY OF THE ELDER

-Section 6-

Elders and the Pastorate

THE MINISTRY OF THE ELDER

THE MINISTRY OF THE ELDER

As Paul wrote concerning spiritual gifts, he said that there were diversities of administrations. Though the Holy Spirit endows men with gifts, individuals can have the same gift and ministry; but how it is administered within the Body of Christ may be different. The same holds true for the Elder.

In the last two sections, we discussed how non-Ruling Elders should serve the pastor and the local church. However, we will turn our attention in these next few sections to the Ruling Elder; that is, the minister who discovers he is called to the office of pastor.

Recognizing the Call

The Servant Elder and/or Evangelist Elder is a candidate for the office of Pastor. This transition in ministry occurs in two ways. Regardless of how the transition is revealed, there are certain protocols, spiritual and natural that need adherence.

The first way an Elder may receive the call to the pastoral office is through *ecclesiastical appointment*, that is, the Bishop recognizes the grace upon an Elder and appoints him as the pastor of a church. Some try to regard this as less "divine" than a personal supernatural revelation of the Holy Spirit. However, this is not the case.

In the Old Testament, Elisha's call to the prophetic office was not recorded as coming to him directly. It was Elijah, under divine instruction that put his mantle upon him.

So he departed thence, and found Elisha the son of Shaphat, who was plowing with twelve yoke of oxen before him, and he with the twelfth: and Elijah passed by him, and cast his mantle upon him. (I Kings 19:19)

THE MINISTRY OF THE ELDER

After this, Elisha recognized that he was called to the prophetic office. The same holds true for some pastors, the revelation for their transition into this ministry may come through revelation given to established leadership.

In the New Testament, the earliest accounts recognize ecclesiastical appointment as an established means of discovering and placing new pastors in the churches. Paul instructed Titus,

> *For this cause left I thee in Crete, that thou shouldest set in order the things that are wanting, and ordain*

THE MINISTRY OF THE ELDER

elders in every city, as I had appointed thee. (Titus 1:5)

After discovering a man's spiritual maturity and wisdom, Titus, as well as Timothy, were instructed to ordain elders the same way that Paul had appointed them and placed them over churches.

The Elder who receives an ecclesiastical appointment is in no way "less called" as an Elder who has received a revelation; which brings us to the second way an Elder received the call to the pastoral office that is, ***divine/personal revelation***.

It is unnecessary to review the numerous biblical accounts of God personally calling an individual to a particular ministry.

As a Bible-believing and Spirit-led institution, C.O.G.I.C. recognizes that personal inspiration and unction of the Holy Spirit does occur.

However, the Elder who receives revelation of a pastoral call through personal revelation or the prophetic ministry of others needs to balance revelation with accountability and submission.

THE MINISTRY OF THE ELDER

Respect Leadership

The Elder who receives a divine/personal call should realize that a call does not release him from accountability to his local pastor and C.O.G.I.C. leadership. After Samuel anointed David as king, we have no record of him gathering an army and deposing Saul. He went back to tending to his father's sheep.

Then Samuel took the horn of oil, and anointed him in the midst of his brethren: and the Spirit of the LORD came upon David from that day

THE MINISTRY OF THE ELDER

forward. So, Samuel rose up, and went to Ramah. (I Samuel 16:13

The Elder must have this same mindset. He must learn how to "yet serve" in the local church, knowing that another ministry awaits him. He must not develop the spirit of Absalom, who wanted to overthrow his father, David.

He must guard against the spirit of rebellion when it is realized that he will lead others. He has to continue to be subject to authority, as his authority will increase.

THE MINISTRY OF THE ELDER

When an Elder receives divine revelation, he should (as much is as possible) speak with his current pastor who may have insight into the timing of this calling as well as other pertinent vital information concerning administrative responsibilities defined by the C.O.G.I.C. organization.

An Elder who plans to start a separate church should not seek to take current members of his church with him. He should **NOT** steal the hearts of men and women to follow him. He should have an established policy in reference to

THE MINISTRY OF THE ELDER

others coming to the proposed new church. Here are three "I Will's" that should be in his policy:

1. I will ask no others to leave their church to join mine.

2. I will encourage those in my current church to stay and serve the local pastor and church.

3. I will only accept transfers by the consent, endorsement, and permission of an individual's current pastor (especially for those coming from other C.O.G.I.C. churches), verbal or written. (also see Official Manual)

This policy will protect the unity of C.O.G.I.C. pastors and leaders. It will protect the Elder from becoming concerned with numbers, rather than souls according to the will of God.

It will also guard the Elder from becoming manipulative and duplicitous in his efforts to establish the new work. In addition, it will place the Elder in a position to trust God for the increase.

Receiving the Appointment

No Elder can appoint himself as an official C.O.G.I.C. pastor of a church governed by the denomination, even one

THE MINISTRY OF THE ELDER

that he has started.

He must follow the established guidelines for starting a ministry under the C.O.G.I.C. banner (see Official Manual). He must make sure he has fulfilled all the required paperwork and organizational documents required by the law and C.O.G.I.C.

Let every soul be subject unto the higher powers. For there is no power but of God: the powers that be are ordained of God. (Romans 13:1)

After these things are in place, he must receive an appointment to the

THE MINISTRY OF THE ELDER

pastoral office by the Bishop. In addition, there are installation services that must be held for the pastor and the new church. These are important as they establish the validity of the new pastor and church. It also identifies this new ministry as a recognized entity within C.O.G.I.C.

Since many parts are involved in the establishing of a new church and appointment of a new pastor, the Elder cannot rely solely upon his personal/divine revelation. He must be in consistent communication with his local pastor who will be able to give guidance

THE MINISTRY OF THE ELDER

and direction.

In addition, the local pastor will serve as the Elder's first public endorser of his ministry. Hence, it has to be stated again, that communication between the Elder and his current pastor is important.

The Elder should in no wise begin a new church without the knowledge and consent of his current pastor. If the Elder feels that is not possible, he should walk orderly and speak with the Superintendent in order that peace will remain and the will of God is accomplished.

THE MINISTRY OF THE ELDER

He should not hold secret religious services and bible studies without the knowledge and consent of his pastor. He should not malign the character and authority of his current pastor to turn the hearts of the congregants toward him.

The Elder should approach this new ministry with prayer, openness, and accountability to his local pastor and C.O.G.I.C. leadership.

THE MINISTRY OF THE ELDER

Ministerial Notes:

_____

_____

_____

_____

_____

_____

_____

_____

THE MINISTRY OF THE ELDER

THE MINISTRY OF THE ELDER

-Section 7-

Basic Protocols for the Ruling Elder

THE MINISTRY OF THE ELDER

Once an Elder receives an ecclesiastical or a divine appointment to the pastoral office, the administration of a new church or an already established church becomes vitally important.

In this section, we want to give basic protocols that must be adhered to whether an Elder is appointed to an established church or if he is beginning a new church. The Official Manual should be consulted regularly.

Seek Counsel

Whether a new or established church, the oversight of a local church is an awesome responsibility. Having godly counsel safeguards the Elder and the people over whom he has the spiritual oversight.

Where no counsel is, the people fall: but in the multitude of counseller there is safety. (Proverbs 11:14)

The Elder who fails to receive godly wisdom and counsel will frustrate the success of the local assembly and the purpose of God. Hence, the reception of counsel from his former pastor, current superintendent, and bishop (if possible) is

THE MINISTRY OF THE ELDER

crucial.

He should speak to those in leadership who know intimately the ordinances of C.O.G.I.C. He should surround himself with other leaders who will pray for him and speak into his life for his personal benefit and the furtherance of the local work.

Have a Vision

For New Churches. The Elder who begins a new church should have a WRITTEN vision, which should govern the spiritual direction of the ministry. Of course, the established vision should not conflict with any of the beliefs held by C.O.G.I.C.

Some reading may not be clear as to what a vision consists of. The **VISION** should consist of the overall vision of the local church, a clearly stated mission statement, and a motto, which gives a capsulated expression of what the ministry is about.

> *And the LORD answered me, and said, Write the vision, and make it plain upon tables, that he may run that readeth it. (Habakkuk 2:2)*

THE MINISTRY OF THE ELDER

Now, we know that the overall vision and mission of any church is to fulfill the great commission of preaching the gospel and making disciples.

However, the local ministry will have specific ways in which to accomplish this; hence, the necessity of a vision, mission, and motto. These will give clarity to the direction of the ministry and keep the pastor and the congregation focused.

It will guard against moving in avenues and directions not given by God for that local church. Below is a quick

THE MINISTRY OF THE ELDER

guide to the overall vision:

1. Vision – Defines the ministry at its peak – It reveals the God-given goal and purpose of the local assembly. It defines what the ministry should achieve over time.

2. Mission – Defines how the ministry will reach its vision. It tells the "who, what, when, and why."

3. Motto – Defines succinctly the overall thrust of the ministry.

The vision of a local church should be able to accommodate the established ministries and auxiliaries

THE MINISTRY OF THE ELDER

already functional in the C.O.G.I.C. denomination. These will help the new minister and church have a foundation for their ministry as they operate within the framework of C.O.G.I.C.

For Established Churches. If an Elder is appointed to an established church, he must not have the attitude of Rehoboam; and go in and change everything. He must first find out if the local church already has an established vision (whether in writing or passed down verbally).

From there, he should seek to establish that vision again in the hearts of

THE MINISTRY OF THE ELDER

the people. If he has received other insight to build upon what has been established, then he must implement these things into the existing vision with wisdom and care.

Legal Accountability

The Elder should be knowledgeable or have access to information regarding all legal matters in the establishment and functioning of a church.

He first must be aware of the state requirements for a church as well as the governing statutes of C.O.G.I.C. The Elder must ensure that the church's bylaws are

THE MINISTRY OF THE ELDER

in place and known among those in leadership in his church.

Accordingly, the bylaws of the local church should be in full harmony with the governing bylaws of C.O.G.I.C. If a pastor discovers after appointment to an established church that bylaws are needed or they need to be updated, he must seek counsel from C.O.G.I.C. leadership. In addition, seek legal counsel that bylaws are biblically sound and legally acceptable.

The Elder must be acquainted with all laws concerning child abuse and under age legal violations. He must have

THE MINISTRY OF THE ELDER

protocols in place to deal with legal matters, if they should arise, occurring under the jurisdiction of the local church.

The Elder should be acquainted with city ordinances with respect to open meetings. He should understand state laws concerning marriage and performing these ceremonies. In addition, he should have access to knowledge of any laws, which may affect the outreach of the local ministry and its ministry operations.

THE MINISTRY OF THE ELDER

Notes:

THE MINISTRY OF THE ELDER

www.ingramcontent.com/pod-product-compliance
Lightning Source LLC
Chambersburg PA
CBHW050341010526
44119CB00049B/650